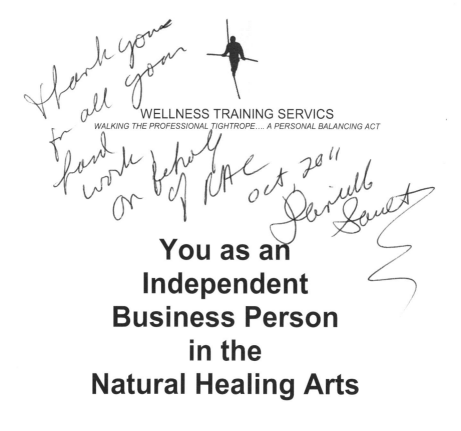

WELLNESS TRAINING SERVICS

WALKING THE PROFESSIONAL TIGHTROPE.... A PERSONAL BALANCING ACT

You as an Independent Business Person in the Natural Healing Arts

How to use your mind to aim for a successful healing arts business.

By R. Danielle Gault

Published by

Wellness Training Services
http://www.wellness-training-services.com
Toronto, ON, Canada

WELLNESS TRAINING SERVICES

Cover picture ©iStockphoto.com/Janne Ahro

INTRODUCTION

We all wish for recognition of our accomplishments although that is not the primary motivator. Recognition for what we do is very satisfying. Often we are our own worst enemies to our success. We need to explore these thoughts and that is what this book is about. What do you really, really want from your accomplishments and what are you willing to do or not do to get that?

Danielle Gault

"It's ill-becoming for an old broad to sing about how bad she wants it. But occasionally we do."
Singer: Lena Horne

This book combines relevant theory with practical insight and tools for running your business. Many people in the natural healing arts field have a challenging time getting their business off the ground or developing their business to the next level.

Some of these challenges can be around the idea of running a business itself or can be around how one feels about taking money for services provided.

This practical book will provide you with insights into your patterns for running your independent business. You will gain:

- A better understanding of yourself and your business

- Improved ability to discuss and satisfy your professional needs

- Enhanced problem-solving abilities

- Greater clarity on how to run your business professionally

ACKNOWLEDGEMENTS

To the many participants and students I've taught over the years and to the wisdom and courage they have taught me. Thank you.

TABLE OF CONTENTS

1

BUSINESS CONCEPTS: MARKETING, SALES, SERVICE

1

BUSINESS CONCEPTS: MARKETING, SALES, SERVICE

The Reflexology Association of Canada strives to upgrade our profession in the business community and the world at large. In their teaching manual, they use the word "professional" to create the idea that Reflexology is a healing arts modality that should be taken seriously by us as practitioners, by our Association as members, by our customers as clients, and by the business community. This is achieved by the way we see and express ourselves.

Whether your healing arts profession is in Reflexology, Energy work, Naturopathic Medicine, Iridology, or Ear Candling, how you see yourself as a healing artist goes a long way in how you set up and provide your services to others.

The objective of this book is to learn to use a variety of tools and insights to improve your business success. Be open to explore and learn and perhaps feel uncomfortable at times. This is how we grow.

Professional business practices can be defined as an exchange. As a society, we are linked to the community through exchanges of goods and services by sharing our talents and products with others for money or for a service or product of perceived equal value.

These exchanges are based on an important principle that we are always striving to satisfy and meet the needs of self and others.

Business services can be defined as a problem-solving process in which customers' needs are identified and met by a company or business person with a product or service to share to the mutual benefit of both parties.

Two main service components that are required to ensure an exchange takes place are:

1. People smarts and skills -- the process of being engaged in serving our clients; and
2. Product or service knowledge -- what the product or service is and how it works to benefit the customer or client.

Of the two service components, people smarts and skills are harder to define and harder to do. This is true because "people smarts and skills" are about a process rather than a tangible item. Processes are alive, dynamic, and are based on how we go about servicing our clients and how that service and exchange takes place. Sometimes, our own people-smarts and skills get in our way of completing a successful exchange.

FOCUS ACTIVITY – RELATING TO CUSTOMERS

Think of a recent incident where you were a customer (perhaps in the healing arts field) and the situation wasn't satisfying for you.

Describe the situation in terms of what you wanted to receive and how the service provider treated you.

What happened? What didn't you like?

_____

_____

_____

_____

_____

_____

_____

Now describe how you felt and reacted. Would you go back to that place of business again? Why or why not?

_____

_____

_____

_____

_____

_____

How would you have wanted to be treated in this situation?

_____

_____

_____

_____

_____

_____

_____

_____

Some terms:

A Professional is defined as someone who is related to or belonging to a profession. Professionalism is defined as someone who is competent or skilled and who can demonstrate their competency and skills at the standards that their profession defines.

In any business exchange, both parties want to feel good about the transaction.

YOU AS THE PROFESSIONAL

As a professional, you want fair compensation for your services. If I give you this 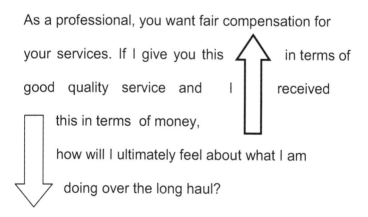 in terms of good quality service and I received this in terms of money, how will I ultimately feel about what I am doing over the long haul?

YOU AS THE CUSTOMER

As a customer, you want a fair exchange for services rendered.

If I pay you this in terms of money and I receive this in terms of service, I most likely will not return for any future exchange.

In any business transaction, both the customer and the service provider want to be honoured and this requires that there is a fair price for good quality service. If you want to stay in the game as a service provider, the exchange principle goes both ways. It is important that you don't sell yourself short as a service provider in the natural healing arts. This is something that this industry and the people in it have often struggled with – putting a fair value on the talents, skills, and experience we have to offer others.

An exchange feels good when both parties feel that the exchange is fair.

BUSINESS CONCEPTS – HOW DO YOU RELATE TO THE FOLLOWING?

- **Marketing:** The process and techniques of promoting, selling and distributing a product or service.
- **Sales:** Giving something in return for something else.
- **Service:** Performing actions auxiliary to production or distribution that contribute to building loyal customers.

Marketing – getting the message out to the targeted audience.

Sales – an exchange.

Service – follow up, pleasant interactions, loyalty and public relations activities that build customer relationships.

A. On a scale of 1 to 5, where 5 is excellent and 1 is poorly expressed, how would you rate yourself – circle your answer.

Marketing	1	2	3	4	5
Sales:	1	2	3	4	5
Service:	1	2	3	4	5

B. Capture your thoughts:

Marketing – I rated myself at _____ rating because:

_____

_____

_____

_____

_____

_____

_____

_____

_____

_____

Sales – I rated myself at _____ rating because:

_____

_____

_____

_____

_____

_____

_____

_____

_____

Service – I rated myself at _____ rating because:

_____

_____

_____

_____

_____

_____

_____

_____

_____

B. Take a few minutes to capture some of your thoughts, insights and surprises.

_____

_____

_____

_____

_____

_____

_____

_____

_____

_____

_____

_____

_____

_____

_____

_____

_____

_____

_____

THINKING ABOUT YOUR BUSINESS

The first step towards improving your professional results is asking yourself some questions about your business. Please answer questions 1 to 4.

Don't panic if you don't know all the answers right now. You're just getting started. However, these questions do provide a great framework for beginning to think realistically about **You as an Independent Business Person in the Natural Healing Arts**.

We will start the process right now but you will most likely have to complete your thinking over time.

Perhaps you will want to stay in touch with other professionals and do some brainstorming, get some feedback, or ask questions to stimulate your thinking. But let's start the process right now.

1. How would you describe the type of industry you are in?

_____

_____

_____

_____

_____

_____

_____

_____

_____

_____

_____

_____

_____

_____

_____

_____

_____

2. How would you describe the purpose of your business in this industry?

_____

_____

_____

_____

_____

_____

_____

_____

_____

_____

_____

_____

_____

_____

3. What is your product or service? Who does it serve and what customers' needs are you filling?

_____

_____

_____

_____

_____

_____

_____

_____

_____

_____

_____

_____

_____

_____

4. In a few paragraphs, write down what makes your business unique.

_____

_____

_____

_____

_____

_____

_____

_____

_____

_____

_____

_____

_____

_____

_____

5. Now, articulate how you would describe what your business does, who it serves, and how it goes about doing this.

Make another attempt and rewrite your statement.

Make another attempt at writing your statement but make it even shorter.

---

6. What are the top three customer objectives to buying your product/service?

_____

_____

_____

_____

_____

_____

_____

_____

_____

_____

_____

_____

7. How does your pricing compare to your competitors? Elaborate on the comparison, the rationale, and the benefits.

_____

_____

_____

_____

_____

_____

_____

_____

_____

_____

_____

_____

_____

_____

_____

_____

_____

8. Do you make special offers? If so, what are they? If you are not making them, are they something you would consider? If so, what would they be?

_____

_____

_____

_____

_____

_____

_____

_____

_____

_____

_____

_____

_____

_____

_____

9. What plans do you have for advertising and
   promotions?

_____

_____

_____

_____

_____

_____

_____

_____

_____

_____

_____

_____

_____

_____

_____

_____

_____

10. What data sheets, brochures, diagrams, sketches, photographs, related press releases, or other documentation about your product or service do you currently have? Is there someone you can share these with and get some feedback from them? If so, who would that be?

_____

_____

_____

_____

_____

_____

_____

_____

_____

_____

_____

_____

_____

_____

_____

_____

11. What thoughts do you have for financing the growth of your business?

_____

_____

_____

_____

_____

_____

_____

_____

Capture any additional thoughts before you leave this section.

_____

_____

_____

_____

_____

_____

_____

_____

2

HOW YOU SEE YOURSELF – HOW YOU SEE YOUR STRENGTHS – YOUR MARKET BASE

2

HOW YOU SEE YOURSELF – HOW YOU SEE YOUR STRENGTHS – YOUR MARKET BASE

Understanding yourself objectively in any given business exchange process can help to clarify what your needs are and how you can use your strengths (and minimize your blind-spots) for growing your business.

Self-awareness increases your ability to deal effectively with every situation and especially with difficult situations where the stakes are high -- such as business exchanges with customers. It is useful to know that what can be a difficult situation to one person can be a highly stimulating and even relaxing experience to someone else. Let's take a look at people differences in order to increase our business skills and strategies.

Sign your signature on the top line (next page) with the hand that you generally write with. Then on the bottom line, sign your signature with the opposite hand – the one you don't generally write with.

_____

_____

WHAT IS A PREFERENCE?

What you will notice is that you can write with both hands but you prefer one over the other. Because that natural preference is there, you used that hand more often and therefore developed that capability. It is easier, more efficient and generally more readable. You can do both, however, and this is the point of the exercise.

Preferences are natural and they are inherent in us. The least developed hand is immature in its utility, takes more energy to concentrate on performing a simple task, and is often child-like in its expression. But remember, you can do both but prefer the one to the other.

27

The concept of how we live our lives applies the same way to how we run our businesses. Some of us prefer a more structured approach and some of us like to go with the flow.

Which one is more like you?

STRUCTURED – are you more:
Of a planner, needing a orderly, organized systematic approach?
Are you wanting clear definitions and limits?
Do you prefer controlling, regulating, completing tasks on time, and having established rules and structures?

Or, do you prefer:

UNSTRUCTURED – are you more:
Spontaneous, flexible, unstructured, messy, go-with-the-flow, without a plan, often appearing disorderly, without limits, usually rushing last minute to complete things, and adapting the rules to fit the situation.

This exercise reflects your orientation to the outside world and refers to the lifestyle or business style that you adopt.

PERSONALITY DYNAMICS

- Personality dynamics is a self-descriptive measure of one's own lifestyle and awareness preferences based on Dr. Carl Gustave Jung's theory of psychological types (1921).
- The self-awareness assessment tool can provide you with a better idea of your strengths as well as your blind spots when managing your business.
- The tool looks at four awarenesses of preferred foci. The awareness that you identify as most like you is called a personality preferences profile.

Please understand that this assessment needs to be treated with skepticism and that the assessment is a tool which:

- Describes preferences not skills or abilities
- Says that all preferences are equally important
- Describes rather than prescribes
- Focuses on strengths and "gifts" of each profile type

WHAT IS MY PREFERENCE?

Seeing our business as a whole system, we can understand that each link in the system makes the system more effective as a whole. Each component of your business is connected to the whole when making business transactions and exchanges. These exchanges allow your business to evolve and to meet the demands and pressures facing it both in the present as well as in the future.

We begin our journey by reviewing people differences through preferences. Preferences are a part of an individual's system and are comprised of how we think, feel, and act. Preferences help us develop our mental software that can be defined as a blueprint outlining our tendencies. What preference is most like you?

Clarifying these tendencies helps us to understand our behaviours and our outcomes. We have the choice to follow these tendencies or to oppose or modify them.

But, living in tune with our own system is what promotes healthier life-long habits, reduces stress, and increases tolerance of others. Think of yourself and your business as a wholistic system consisting of an equilateral triangle composed of:

The whole system at work.

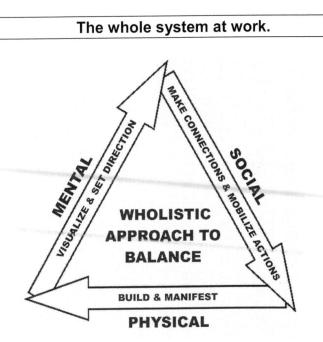

- The mental side – Ideas, Objective, Overview, Systems, Expectations, Infinite

- The social side – Actions, Reactions, Connections, Coordination, Cooperation, Communication

- The physical side – Manifestation, Concrete, Detailed, Tangible, Parameters, Finite, Feedback

Each side of this triangle is of equal importance and when one side is affected, the whole system is affected.

Although we all think (Mental awareness), feel (Social awareness), and do (Physical awareness), we use these awarenesses in different proportions attempting to develop our strengths by staying in our most preferred awareness the longest. When we use our preferred awareness often, we develop that awareness and it becomes easily accessible to us.

Which preference is most like you? Designed to assist you in developing a congruent business relations style that best supports your natural tendencies, marshals your talents, as well as increases your opportunity to effectively share them with others, is what personal preferences is about.

Being aware of and developing all of your functions, i.e., turning the dial up on those tendencies that are least preferred by you, can increase your tolerance and capacity for interacting with others.

These awarenesses or preferences can be thought of as the four basic elements that make up our planet – air, fire, water, and earth and can be defined as follows:

THE MENTAL AWARENESS -- AIR -- OPERATES AS **THE DREAMER** in us: The AIR part of us is what carries us through when times get tough. The AIR provides us with our life's purpose or our dream in life of what life means to us. Even when we feel that life is a bit rough, the AIR element can lift us up and pull us through. As the objective part of ourselves, our mental awareness receives intuitive information that we then analytically and logically attempt to organize. This part of our awareness sees the overview, general structures and establishes our values.

THE SOCIAL-MENTAL AWARENESS -- FIRE -- OPERATES AS **THE REALIST** in us: The FIRE part of us actively connects ideas with resources to work through obstacles and overcome the barriers to our dreams. Through an interactive process, working through obstacles becomes easier, thereby ensuring and supporting our ongoing dream achievement as we build our self-confidence along the way. As the social-mental objective part of ourselves, this social awareness keeps us motivated by striving to connect the ideas to people and things through actions.

THE SOCIAL-PHYSICAL AWARENESS -- WATER -- OPERATES AS **THE CATALYST** in us: The WATER part of us is the most subjective and is the subtle, inner most part which strives to make connections with people and resources to keep us enthusiastic about our life. As the social-physical subjective side of ourselves, this social awareness strives to keep us enthusiastic through ongoing support and learning from each other as we develop our human potential.

THE PHYSICAL AWARENESS -- EARTH -- OPERATES AS **THE CRITIC** in us: The EARTH is that part of us that lets us know what obstacles are blocking us from achieving our dreams in life. We feel tension in our bodies when we miss our deadlines or when we do not have enough money, time, or other resources to complete our tasks. We come to appreciate these parameters as we learn to experience them through the feedback in our bodies. As the practical side of us, the physical gross sense perceptions of hearing, seeing, touching, smelling, and tasting strive to be practical by building, making, doing and manifesting tangible results in the physical world.

SELF IDENTIFICATION ACTIVITY

On the next page is a summary of all four temperament groups.

Please read over the four preferences and identify the one that best describes your "natural fit."

You should feel that the preference you select is about 70% accurate in terms of describing your tendencies. Read over the four descriptions quickly and see which profile resonates the closest to how your see yourself.

MENTAL AWARENESS / DREAMERS / AIR
- IS VISIONARY.
- VALUES KNOWLEDGE AND COMPETENCY.
- ENJOYS CREATING MODELS.
- ENGAGES IN LOGICAL REASONING.
- IS SKEPTICAL, ANALYTICAL, AND SELF-CRITICIZING.

SOCIAL-MENTAL AWARENESS / REALISTS / FIRE
- WANTS TO MAKE AN IMPACT.
- NEEDS FREEDOM TO ACT ON IMPULSE.
- IS MOTIVATED TO DO THINGS THAT ARE EXCITING (RIGHT NOW).
- RESPONDS TO WHAT IS CURRENTLY HAPPENING.
- IS A RISK TAKER.
- FOCUSES ON THE PRESENT.

SOCIAL-PHYSICAL AWARENESS / CATALYSTS / WATER
- HIGHLY VALUES PERSONAL RELATIONSHIPS.
- STRIVES TO MAINTAIN OWN INDIVIDUALITY.
- BELIEVES IN OWN IDEALS.
- HAS ABILITY TO GET OTHERS INVOLVED.
- TREATS OWN VISION AS REAL FOR THE MOMENT.
- DOES THINGS FOR THE GREATER GOOD OF SOCIETY.

PHYSICAL AWARENESS / CRITICS / EARTH
- VIEWS LOGISTICS (HOW AND WHEN THINGS GET DONE) AS IMPORTANT.
- HOLDS MAINTAINING THE ORGANIZATION AS IMPORTANT.
- REGARDS EFFICIENCY AS IMPORTANT.
- WANTS TO FOLLOW THE RULES.
- HAS A HIGH NEED FOR SECURITY.
- NEEDS TO PROVIDE SERVICE.
- FOCUSES ON EXPERIENCE, HOW THINGS HAVE WORKED BEFORE.

A. Now, capture your thoughts on the significant points for you of each preference and how you have worked with them throughout your life.

B. Which preference is the most developed and easily accessible for you?

C. How do you know this? What feedback have people given you in the course of your life that tells you this is so?

D. Which preference do you struggle with the most? How does this show up in your life?

Mental Awareness – Dreamers -- Air

_____

_____

_____

_____

_____

_____

_____

_____

_____

Social-Mental – Realists -- Fire

_____

_____

_____

_____

_____

_____

_____

_____

Social-Physical – Catalysts -- Water

_____

_____

_____

_____

_____

_____

_____

_____

Physical -- Critics -- Earth

_____

_____

_____

_____

_____

_____

_____

_____

Next, take a moment and answer the following question:

How is my least developed function getting in my way of developing my business?

_____

_____

_____

_____

_____

_____

_____

3

MONEY AND YOU. WHAT DOES IT MEAN TO YOU? TO YOUR BUSINESS?

3

**MONEY AND YOU. WHAT DOES IT MEAN TO YOU?
TO YOUR BUSINESS?**

Let's think about money as a metaphor for our energy and tie that energy to our business. Being self-employed forces you in many ways to attach your time, expertise, and experience to money. What does money mean to you?

Definition of money: A medium of exchange.

Definition of wealth: Your assets far out weigh your liabilities.

Definition of rich people: Owning much money and property – having an abundance of wealth.

Exercise – Money and You -- Sit in a relaxed position, let your mind wander and answer the following:

1. For me, money is _____

2. For me, money is_____

3. For me, wealth is_____

4. For me, wealth is_____

5. For me, wealthy people are _____

6. For me, wealthy people are_____

Many people say that our inner game has to be congruent with our outer game in order to produce the results we want and are comfortable having. How much money do you want?

Next, draw a picture of the size of the container you have internally that holds the money you would like to have.

Compare it to what you think a rich person's container would look like and then write your thoughts about the differences.

My Current Container: **A Rich Person's Container:**

How different are these containers?

This exercise is designed to tap into your belief system about money. Capture your insights and thoughts about the size of your container.

_____

_____

_____

_____

_____

What size container do you want in order to be as fulfilled as you would like to be in your life? My new container would look like this:

How would you replace some of your old beliefs about money and your thoughts of limitations about earning money as a healing artist if you could?

Understanding the psychology of money requires a look at Industrial Psychology 101 -- needs-based behaviours.

NEEDS-BASED BEHAVIOURS

Abraham Maslow, an Industrial Psychologist, theorized that all people share certain basic needs. Maslow said that we can't satisfy higher-level needs until lower-level needs are satisfied. For example, our need for friendship would not be a major need until and unless we have satisfied our need for food and shelter.

Maslow said that we can categorize these needs as follows:

1. **SECURITY/SAFETY:** Physical needs consisting of Physiological Needs (food, shelter), followed by Security Needs (protection, order).

2. **AFFILIATION:** Social Needs consisting of a Sense of Belonging and Love (friendship, affection).

3. **POWER:** Social Needs also include the need for Recognition and Respect (success and prestige)

4. **LEARNING:** Mental Needs deal with Self-Actualization, the need to reach our full potential.

We all have these four basic needs striving to be satisfied. When not satisfied, they create tension in us. This tension is designed to motivate us to take action in order to remove the tension by satisfying the need.

Once we have satisfied the need, however, the motivator ceases to be motivating. For example, if we are not hungry and, in fact have eaten too much, such as at a holiday feast, food doesn't provide much of a motivator for us.

When we apply these same motivators to our relationship with money, we can see that money is an expression of our life flow and can be a great tool for spiritual enlightenment in which our struggles, fears, and anxieties about money assist us in seeing clearly what we need to do to evolve.

It is amazing how life straightens out once we get a grip on our attitude and management of money. -- Anonymous

How do you see your money management attitude as it applies to your business? Do you have a positive framework or a negative framework? Which one is more like your framework?

REALISTS -- Positive Side	**DREAMERS -- Positive Side**
Gets the job done quickly. Sees and does. Focuses on goals, not necessarily costs. Can save and spend easily. Can pass money around freely, as long as he/she wants to.	Gets the job done conscientiously. Sees and is responsive after focusing on problem, looking for best cost-effective solutions. Spends money wisely after considering everyone's needs.
Need – Motivated By: Industry, Recognition, Respect. Acts independently but can be inspiring -- benefit is quick, fast.	**Need – Motivated By:** Learning, growing, striving. Acts interdependently. Benefit is personal and performance development.
CRITICS -- Positive Side	**CATALYSTS -- Positive Side**
Can save for the future. Can build wealth and security. Can apply judgment to spending.	Very generous with others. Highly responsive to other's needs. Spends selflessly when sees needs.
Need -- Motivated By: Protection, Order, Safety. Acts dependently due to enjoying being associated with a group/family/team.	**Need -- Motivated By:** A sense of belonging, wanting friendship. Acts dependently -- likes to be liked and creates a friendly environment.

Antagonistic, Opposition, Adverse

Responsive, Sensitive, Understanding

Yielding, Giving In, Passive

Antagonistic, Opposition, Adverse

Responsive, Sensitive, Understanding

REALISTS -- Negative Side

$ - Takes for self with little regard for others. Takes resources without replenishing. Can be reckless and irresponsible. When push comes to shove, takes care of him/herself. Can spend unwisely or save well, either way, self-interest drives most behaviours.

Need -- Motivated By: Power, ego.

Reactions? Pull away or get angry.

Acts independently.

DREAMERS -- Negative Side

$ - Sets standards too high. Can withdraw from others if others don't see the vision as important. Could appear arrogant, aloof, abstract. Could be too challenging and difficult to reach their financial goals.

Need -- Motivated By: Self- regulatory body, never satisfied. Ever striving.

Reactions? Discouraged, you feel like a failure.

Acts interdependently until abandons you -- then independently.

CRITICS -- Negative Side

$ - Hoards for the most part. Self-sacrifices and then justifies not spending. Sometimes it is painful to spend money at all. Gets black and white about spending or saving -- no middle ground. Self-serving, calculating and secretive.

Need -- Motivated By: Safety, security.

Reactions? Pull away or get angry.

Acts dependently -- needs you to sponge off.

CATALYSTS -- Negative Side

$ - Forgets to put self into the equation. Self-sacrifices and then feels like a martyr to the needs of others. Gives money away and gets left holding the bag -- gets taken advantage of by others. Self-serving.

Need -- Motivated By: Wanting to be liked.

Reactions? Pull away, placing little value on exchange.

Acts dependently -- needs you in order to feel good about self.

Where we all want to develop and grow as we work our businesses providing services in exchange for money, is to move to the Performing Stage of getting results. This takes problem-solving strategies, insights, and determination.

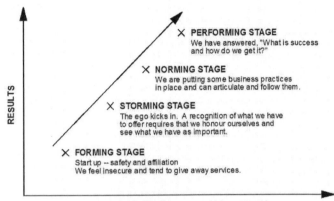

RESULTS

X **PERFORMING STAGE**
We have answered, "What is success and how do we get it?"

X **NORMING STAGE**
We are putting some business practices in place and can articulate and follow them.

X **STORMING STAGE**
The ego kicks in. A recognition of what we have to offer requires that we honour ourselves and see what we have as important.

X **FORMING STAGE**
Start up -- safety and affiliation
We feel insecure and tend to give away services.

DEVELOPING MATURE CUSTOMER RELATIONSHIPS
where exchanges are mutually beneficial

Take a moment and decide what stage in your problem-solving business development you are at.

Check off which stage you are at present:

_____**Forming Stage**

_____**Storming Stage**

_____**Norming Stage**

_____**Performing Stage**

I want/need to move to the next stage and that, for me, would be the _____stage.

51

4

IMPROVING RESULTS USING A PROBLEM-SOLVING APPROACH

4

IMPROVING RESULTS USING A PROBLEM-SOLVING APPROACH

DEVELOPING YOUR BUSINESS:

We all long to get to the Performing Stage in our businesses and that takes being honest with ourselves, commitment on what we have to change in order to develop to the next level and passion to keep us inspired.

Developing your business is a problem-solving process in which we identify where we are and identify where we wish to go and the problem is the gap between those two identifications.

We can use the same problem-solving process when we think about the services we provide and how to work with our clients' needs.

A client comes to us with a problem to solve. We have a service to provide. Once the customers' needs are identified and met by a person with a product or service to share and the gap is closed, the customer and the service provider feel satisfied and there is a mutual benefit for both parties.

The "problem" is defined as the gap between what the customer currently has and what they want for themselves.

FUTURE OUTCOME TO BE ACHIEVED FOR A CLIENT *-- PERHAPS IT IS TO DECREASE PAIN IN THE HIP AND GET CLIENT MORE MOBILE*

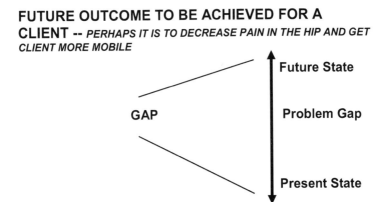

CURRENT REALITY BEING EXPERIENCED *– VERY PAINFUL HIP AND AN INABILITY TO WALK*

Our job is to close the gap. Now, we know that in many healing arts professions one cannot diagnose, prescribe or treat for specific conditions. However, we can speak about tension and stress and indicate that many stressful conditions in the body are balanced with improved circulation and reduction of tension. We can also speak about the effects that some of our clients have experienced. If pain in the hip is the current reality, the present state of our client's imbalance, closing the gap would mean we reduce the pain through circulation work and by putting our client into a relaxed state where the body's natural intelligence can facilitate balance creating the possibility that this will facilitate an increase in the mobility of our client. It is not our job to say that we will get the client more mobile. Our job is to provide the service and monitor the results.

Besides your technical skills and expertise, your job is to:

1. Obtain information on our customer's present situation.
2. Gather information on what the customer's desired situation would be.
3. Once we have identified the gap between the customer's current situation and their desired future situation, then we can propose a plan to close the gap, thus assisting them in solving their problem.

Using this same approach for our business development and closing the gap between staying in the Forming Stage and moving to the Storming Stage, we may be required to tap into our Fire element to cause some things to change.

In marketing our business and closing the gap in terms of moving from Forming to Storming, for example, we can step out and be more assertive in our approach for marketing our services in order to close our business gap. We can make more professional brochures, give talks at various organizations such as at the Better Business Bureau, and offer seasonal specials.

Professionalism is about marketing, selling, and providing ongoing customer service. We must continuously deal with people, persuading and motivating them to buy from our company or business. Becoming a student of human behaviour is critical to every effective business transaction.

Needs-based service works on the premise that people will feel good about a business exchange from you when two conditions have been met. The first condition is that they have a need. The second condition is that you can satisfy that need.

To summarize customer service, the customer relations strategy is as follows:

☐ Act as a problem solver

☐ Be willing to assist the customer in learning about the service you provide.

☐ Get clear about the customer's problem – what is it they are striving to satisfy?

☐ Be willing to demonstrate the benefits of your service to show how it helps the customer address his/her problem and address his/her need.

☐ If there is no need, there is no problem and hence you have nothing to offer because there is nothing to satisfy – there is no gap, no tension.

☐ If there is a need, a problem to solve, you have something to offer and you should proceed accordingly.

Within this premise, your job is to engage in the needs-based problem-solving process by:

1. Determining if there is a need by gathering as much information as possible about your customer's needs and,

2. Proving that your product or service can satisfy the needs your customer disclosed to you.

Motivation theory indicates that we move on things when we have tension and stress and we long to remove this tension and stress from our bodies and minds.

It can help to know that in stressful situations, according to Dr. Carl Jung, without tension, there would be no energy and consequently no personality. This tension is the very essence of life. Without it there would be need to change, to grow, to adapt. We all need some stress and some tension -- just how much is the question.

When In Stressful Situations, Think Rubber Band!

Too stressed, we snap. Not enough stress, we get bored, listless, dull.

Problem-solving skills are at the heart of professional business processes. Problem solving helps uncover information, manage emotions and objections, gets the client involved, and provides structure and meaning to the entire process called needs-based selling.

Everything you say and leave unsaid has an effect on your results. To be effective in running your business, every transaction ought to represent a fair exchange with a customer between what you have to offer and what they are willing to pay. This part of the workshop shows how to appear congruent and focused in what you think, how you feel, and how you act.

A pro-active problem-solving approach to being an independent business person in the Natural Healing Arts Field is not about stopping our thoughts and reactions to these transactions. It is not about putting a lid on the pressure that some of our thoughts about making money through our healing arts work can make us feel. If we try to do these things, we can become mentally or physically dysfunctional and diminish our business activities therefore affecting our bottom line.

Let's work on closing the gap between your current business reality and your future dream or expectation. Pro-active strategies are about redirecting the pressure or energy that we attach to money and our business into something positive by redirecting our thoughts and focusing on positive pro-active actions. First of all, we have to identify the problem. Take a moment and think about what is in your way to producing the results you are after.

Identify: **What is the problem?**

What prevents me from increasing my business activities and reaching the wealth I desire as a result of providing my products and services to others is:

_____

_____

_____

The Mental Side

REFRAMING OUR BELIEFS AND IDEAS ABOUT BUSINESS AND MONEY

One of the best strategies for understanding money and business is to ask yourself, *"IF I COULD HAVE IT ANY WAY I WANT IT, HOW WOULD THAT BE?"*

Imagine you have a magic wand and write down everything you would really, really want if you could have it.

_____

_____

_____

_____

_____

_____

_____

_____

_____

_____

_____

_____

_____

_____

_____

_____

The Physical Side
USING THE CRITICS VOICE, ANSWER THE FOLLOWING:

Because we are driven by our own needs-based behaviour, the Critic in us will say, *"You can't have this dream because…"*

Write down everything that comes to mind that would prevent you from having your dream.

_____

_____

_____

_____

_____

_____

_____

_____

_____

_____

_____

_____

_____

_____

_____

_____

The Social Side

MAKING POSITIVE CONNECTIONS TO ACHIEVE YOUR DREAM

Making connections, communicating and coordinating services.

Take your obstacles and barriers that you generated using the Critic's voice in you and turn the obstacles now into stepping stones.

Come up with at least three next steps to take to make your dreams a reality. Share these steps with someone and ask for support in following through. If one of your obstacles was that you lacked confidence in spreading the word about your unique service, then the social side of you would say:

Critic: I lack confidence in my ability to spread the word about my services.

Realists: Keep spreading the word and your confidence with grow.

For every obstacle that the Critic comes up with, write the stepping stone that the Realist in you would say by turning the obstacle into the stepping stone.

Obstacle #1:

_____

_____

_____

Realist's Response:

_____

_____

_____

_____

Obstacle #2:

_____

_____

_____

Realist's Response:

_____

_____

_____

_____

Obstacle #3:

_____

_____

_____

Realist's Response:

_____

_____

_____

_____

Obstacle #4:

_____

_____

_____

Realist's Response:

_____

_____

_____

_____

A Spiritual saying goes: "We have to do it alone and we can't do it by ourselves." Using our Social side, specifically the Social-Physical, we ask for assistance from others. We live in a world with others and we do need others to further our growth. With others involved, we are more assured that we will manifest our dream. Who or what else do you need in order to close the gap between your current reality and the dream or outcome you wish to achieve? When will you do this? Use the Social-Physical-Catalyst-Water side of yourself to address this factor:

WHO	WHAT	WHEN

The Social Awareness is that part of us that is concerned with connections and relationships. It is the part of us that is more personal, that knows and values the world of connections, that needs communication and offers it, that knows how to collaborate, and the one that organizes and synthesizes. The creative use of ideas and people belongs to the Social Awareness side of us.

By using our Social Awareness, we develop the skills for interacting with others. When working with others, we can sometimes feel frustration and loss of control due to the differences in personalities involved. To prevent poor customer service relations, it is important to counteract negative circumstances. No matter what the situation is, always remain calm, stay constructive, and ask for clarification. When we get the information, we can address the topic in objective and meaningful ways.

Summary

Understanding how we can improve our business as independent business people requires that we think of our self as professionals offering our service and products for a fair and equal exchange where both parties feel satisfied.

Never give up; keep going even when it seems that you are spinning your wheels. Ask for help, support, and stay empowered. Use each side of your human system as follows:

Mental Side: Stay objective and strive to get clarity. Ask, "What can I learn from this and how can I make it work?"

Social Side: Discuss unusual stressful situations with colleagues so they can assist you; stop the "I have to" and reframe to "I want to"; create positive energy around yourself by staying in a problem-solving frame of mind.

Physical Side: Set limits on the number of events you deal with and learn to say no; take care of your body through exercise, diet, sleep, and relaxation techniques.

Keep developing your self-understanding and take care of yourself along the way! If you don't do this, there is only one end in sight – poor health.

> *Remember:*
> *If work is so important and so serious, while leisure*
> *Is not so important and not so serious, then also learn*
> *to do nothing seriously as well.*

We have a swimming pool so we entertain a lot in the summer.

Our SP (FIRE) guests always grab all the pool toys, head right for the water, and invent a new game.

The NF (WATER) guests sprawl on the lounge chairs and talk earnestly about life and people.

The NT (AIR) guests dangle their feet in the water, rib each other, and critique the issues and people in their professions.

And the SJ (EARTH) guests always, always find some work to do, like hanging up towels, husking corn, scrubbing the grill, or pulling weeds from the garden.

■ *Adapted From Type Talk by Otto Kroeger and Janet Thusen.*

SP – stands for Sensing Perceiving in the Myers Briggs Type Indicator (MBTI®)
NF – stands for iNtuitive Feeling in the MBTI®
NT – stands for iNtuitive Thinking in the MBTI®
SJ – stands for Sensing Judging in the MBTI®

To learn more about the Myers-Briggs Type Indicator® and Temperament theory, read Otto Kroeger's book.

Or, contact Danielle Gault at Wellness Training Services at: www.wellness-training-services.com.

APPENDICES

WRITINGS ON TEMPERAMENT STYLES

APPENDIX I

SPIRITUALITY, YOU AND MONEY $

By Danielle Gault

LOOKING AT MONEY AS ENERGY EXCHANGE

Years ago I attended a Money and You Workshop because I felt that money is an expression of spiritual life. Money represents energy and energy fulfills things through beliefs, values and actions. How we think, feel, and handle our money is a direct reflection of how we position ourselves in this finite physical world. Since we are physical beings made of the earth, we are drawn to things of the earth. Food, shelter, clothing, power; these finite things put restrictions on us, causing us some inner tension. When there is tension, there is dynamism along with the opportunity to make decisions that can shape and reshape our lives. If we are wise, we use this tension or inner struggle for making good decisions around the accumulation, management, and use of our energy and our money. But why, then, do some people find themselves constantly in debt while other people hoard their money?

FOUR PERSONALITY PATTERNS

Personality patterns can provide a format for developing self-awareness of how we use our energy. For example, in the Money and You Workshop, there was an experiential exercise where we had so much time and so many pieces of paper that represented money that we could use any way we saw fit. After the exercise, we counted what we had and the person who had the most pieces of paper money won. I had the most money at the end of the exercise not because I was hoarding but because of what I did. Here's what I did; I sat and offered to give people a Reflexology treatment, something I am trained to do and something I love to do.

While performing my services, one participant offered to be my manager. I agreed and he proceeded to sell my services to others, taking his commission for my services from the fee charged. I was doing what I naturally enjoyed doing and he was doing what he naturally enjoyed doing which was marketing. I had the most money when the exercise ended mainly because I didn't have time to spend any money. My manager, because he went around the room, spent some of his money to engage others in my service, living the idea that it takes money to make money. The spiritual lesson

I took from this exercise was: *do what you love to do in the service of others and money will flow your way.*

We can think of ourselves as a three-sided triangle with each side as important as the others. There is the Mental Side, the Social Side, and the Physical Side – all three sides create a holistic dynamic system that is as strong as each side or as weak as each side. Although we all have these three sides of ourselves, we tend to prefer one side over the others thereby creating a dominant expression. As we go through life, we may or may not understand that all sides need to be developed. We also need to understand that sometimes the development of our one-sided preference may be too strong for someone else which can cause tension and conflict.

Following is a brief description of these three sides with the Social expression taking two forms. Through many years of learning, developing, and delivering personality workshops, I clearly see how these four patterns of human expressions often play out and I can relate these patterns to how people may show up around the topic of their money.

1. **PHYSICAL:** Some people focus more on security and safety needs while conserving energy and seeking stability in the physical world which I relate to the element of earth.

2. **SOCIAL-PHYSICAL:** Other people focus more on relationship building, harmony, feelings and the social world of empathetically connecting with others which I relate to the element of water. The Social-Physical is more subjective rather than objective.

3. **SOCIAL-MENTAL:** Still others focus more on distilling complicated topics into bullet points, solving immediate problems and connecting the world of ideas to immediate actions with and, through others, moving ideas forward, which I relate to the element of fire. The Social-Mental is more objective rather than subjective.

4. **MENTAL:** And there are people who focus more on ideas, systems, ovorviews and the mental world of inventing and creating new ways to view things which I relate to the element of air.

OPPORTUNITIES FOR REFLECTION

Struggles with money indicate opportunities for reflection in learning how to use money as a tool for spiritual discernment. For example, recently we had four different visitors to our summer home in New Zealand. Having a home in New Zealand and being on a fixed income was a new experience and as New Zealand is a long journey, we started having long-term visitors, something else we were not use to. Our struggle was how to receive people while honouring each others' parameters – theirs and ours.

PHYSICAL - EARTH: One visitor expressed himself as the earth element which can be characterized by more inwardness, not as chatty as some of the other elements; a slower pace, and a deliberate, thoughtful approach to spending. As time with this person and his wife wore on, we noticed they never offered to pay for gas nor chip in for groceries. When we went out to eat, they meagerly ordered for themselves while eating our leftovers. We knew these people had a decent nest-egg, a good pension, and were debt-free; something an earth element person would clearly strive for in their need for building wealth and security.

Our resentment grew as we began counting the days to their departure. We choose not to address the situation at the time of their visit because we were afraid we would say something we might regret and because we felt certain that some reciprocity would show up eventually. It never did.

Because they were relatives that we've known for many years, we did not want our resentment to get in the way of our connection with them. A few months later we decided to call and ask if they were having financial difficulties as they appeared to be concerned about spending money while visiting us. They said no they were not concerned about money but that they had put themselves on a budget.

Staying with us for two weeks helped subsidize their vacation but did nothing for our pocketbook; and their explanation did nothing to warm the cockles of our hearts. We determined that in honouring ourselves, we needed to be more upfront with our visitors.

This couple's relationship with money showed what Benjamin Franklin said – *he that is of the opinion money will do everything may well be suspected of doing everything for money.*

SOCIAL-PHYSICAL-WATER: Another set of visitors were more the water element expression. We knew that the husband, now in his mid-seventies, had had a round of unfortunate financial set backs and the likelihood of getting financially on his feet was slim. Typical of the water person, in striving to serve others, he and his wife wanted to pay for more than their share. And in our concern for them, we looked for ways to buy food and gas when they were not around.

During their visit, using feng shui, they prepared our house for re-sale which resulted in an excellent offer within a few days. After the house sold, we sent our friends a $500 cheque that we called a marketing fee.

They resisted, but we insisted and thanked them for their service. Billy Graham said -- *if a person gets his attitude toward money straight, it will help straighten out almost every other area in his life.*

We hope this couple in their service to others will keep some wealth for themselves.

SOCIAL-MENTAL-FIRE: When our third visitor, a closer relative and someone I am more familiar with, came I, perhaps a little too zealously, wanted to be straightforward about money. After the first two visitors, I longed to bring up the discussion from the start and proceeded to propose a system for sharing expenses. He wanted nothing to do with my system and said things would work out.

I would say that this person represented the fire element because, as is typical of fire people, they often find themselves at the starting gate revving to get into the race. Never remaining too long on any one track, they can be seen going from race track to race track which can also be true in their partnerships. As this was his third marriage, we had to get use to another wife. Fire people are constantly starting over as they get disillusioned by others. When this happens, they seek out a solution to relieve their inner tension. Never comfortable with inner tension for very long, their life appears to be that of solving one problem after another.

Once their force is released in whatever context they are in, peoples' wills are usually bent in their direction.

And so, thrown upon myself and sometimes confused when it came to opening the purse, I seemed to have no choice; we were going to do it his way. The thing about fire people is that there is never a dull moment. Everything you do with them is faster than a speeding bullet. When things don't go their way, however, their internal tension, expressed outwardly, comes across as overpowering.

Fire element people live to solve problems and if there are no immediate problems, they seem to create them. Unlike the earth element person who strives for profound stability and the least expenditure of energy, fire people seem to constantly expend energy.

Their spiritual struggle in life is that they forget to build down, living their life so much in the present tense. Being inclined this way because they fail to learn from past experiences, they tend to go through resources quickly. As they are never satisfied with what they have, they can take, grab, use, and often fail to replenish. When this happens, other people often feel left behind in a cloud of smoke wondering what just happened.

So I gave up my need to have a system and trusted that our visitor's way of dealing with money would be fair

– which by the way, it was. We had a good time because he and his partner enjoyed everything we did. We spent money doing just exactly what we all wanted to do, and they were always upbeat. So, once I let go of my struggle to have a system, I lived out of his system and Robert Frost's saying – *Never ask of money spent where the spender thinks it went. Nobody was ever meant to remember or invent what he did with every cent.*

MENTAL-AIR: Our last visitors were people we didn't know very well. I determined the husband to be an air element expression because I found myself acting a little more formally when around him. This happens to me when I experience politeness and stillness of movement -- something he expressed. We didn't discuss money because there seemed no pressure to get the question of shared expenses out into the open.

He and his wife were polite and considerate and our discussions tended to be more around world issues and planetary problems in the bio-geo-sphere. Although the time together went quickly, I don't remember too much laughter and certainly no problems but a great deal of civility.

Air element people tend to be like clouds. They are present, you can see them, but then they disappear. The can be formal, detached, and conceptual. Drawn toward the world of ideas, they live in a creative flow of future possibilities. A natural disdain for disagreement coupled with a need for recognition of their competencies, the air element person is not easy to know often because their standards are too high for the rest of us to achieve.

Not wanting to lower their standards in any context, they would not work just for money but to bring something new into the realm of possibility.

They would tend to see money as Ayn Rand did – *Ask yourself – did you get your money by fraud, by pandering to men's vices, by lowering your standards, by doing work you despise for purchases you scorn? If so, then your money will not give you a penny's worth of joy.*

STRUGGLES WITH MONEY – WHERE ARE YOU?

Our visitors came and went and we carried on preparing for our journey back to Canada amazed at the differences in the people we hosted. Seeing people from an elemental expression of air, fire, water, and earth helped us to understand and broaden our responses to our guests as well as temper our reactions.

As flowers require different amounts of sunlight, water, soil, and nourishment, people require different ways of interacting and this is especially true when dealing with money issues.

Using the elements, we can shed light on our use of money by how it flows in and out of our lives. Does it flow out too quickly or do we hold on to it too tightly? Struggles with money – where are you?

1. Earth people are never secure in the feeling of having enough money. To spiritually expand their view of themselves, they need to loosen up and spread their money around more.

2. To develop spiritually, fire people need to decide to hold on to their money because their money comes in and goes out quickly. Unless they stop

and manage this flowing process, they never gain wealth and if they do, they lose it only to rebuild it and lose it again.

3. Water people, in order to expand themselves, need to put themselves in the equation when it comes to money as they tend to put others first.

4. And air people don't pay much attention to things of the earth but prefer to work out systems while floating in abstraction. They prefer to avoid mundane topics that seem insignificant to them but which could increase their connections to others if they show more interest. Unless working with money for achieving something worthwhile, money discussions are not a favorite topic with this group.

AN EXPRESSION OF OUR LIFE FLOW

Money is not the root of all evil but can shed light on some of our struggles in how we spend and use our energy. How we handle our money is really a direct reflection of how we think, feel and act. It is our energy; an expression of our life flow.

An anonymous writer said – *Money can't buy friendship – friendship must be earned. Money can't buy a clear conscience – square dealing is the price tag. Money can't buy the glow of good health – right living is the secret. Money can't buy happiness – happiness is a mental condition. Money can't buy a good character – good character is achieved through decent habits of private living and wholesome dealings in our open contacts with our fellow men.*

Because money can be a great tool for spiritual enlightenment, we can see money as adrenaline for our soul in which our struggles, fears, and anxieties about money assist us in seeing clearly what we need to do to evolve. It's amazing how life straightens out once we get a grip on our attitude and management of money.

PERSONALITY PATTERNS – POSITIVE AND NEGATIVE ATTRIBUTES AND MONEY MANAGEMENT			
Detail-oriented	Tries to connect the dots	Leads others and others follow	Comes up with the overviews and improves systems
Patient	Empathetic	Quick and forceful	One-pointed and focused on vision
Plodding – systematic	Is flexible and can jump from one action item to another	Works in a trial-and-error method looking for the next solution	Feeds ideas outward for the sake of ideas and happy to leave the details to others
Methodical	Multi-tasker	Great delegators when moving projects forward	Works independently stimulated by ideas
Draws on the past	Draws on the past, present, and future to ensure relating to the whole picture	Draws on the present focusing quickly on the next set of action items	Draws on future possibilities and improvements
Works for others	Connects others together	Connects ideas to next immediate actions	Generates new ideas, inventions, systems
Good with saving money and generating wealth	Gives money freely to others	Spends what needs to be spent to get the job done	Uses money enthusiastically for new ideas and investments they believe in
Positive EARTH Negative	**Positive WATER Negative**	**Positive FIRE Negative**	**Positive AIR Negative**
Stubborn	Murky	Dominating	Distant and aloof
Judgmental	Confusing	Over powering	Abstract
Too slow	Too scattered	Too fast – misses nuances	Low tolerance for disturbances
Closed minded	Lacks boundaries	Steps on toes	Not interested in people's emotional problems
Long-standing suffering due to feeling taken for granted by others	Martyred and can be misused by others	Insensitive and may be avoided by others	Not understood and can be abandoned by others
Hoarding for the sake of hoarding	Overly generous and forgets to include oneself in the equation	Spends, takes, and forgets to replenish	Short-sighted, seeing money only as a resource to satisfy their next idea

84

APPENDIX II

PERSONALITIES AT WORK

APPENDIX II

PERSONALITIES AT WORK

The MBTI® indicates specific differences for ways we would like to behave in the world. The world, however, imposes its own game plan on us and often has counter expectations for our behaviours.

These opposite expectations have inherent in them -- tensions. According to Dr. Carl Jung, the tension of opposites is the very essence of life itself. Without tension, there would be no energy and consequently no personality. All personality types experience stress when dealing with conflict, and therefore, an understanding of our own way of dealing with conflict, combined with conflict management insights can help us to produce more effective results for dealing with tensions when the world doesn't conform to our expectations.

A CASE STUDY

For example, a company I consulted with had as its president an independent business man who didn't think much of emotions -- he was an ENTP. The wife, co-partner in the company, was an ISFP. She did not want to deal with anything that was unpleasant. She buffered all unpleasantness in the organization and virtually negated its existence. The husband/president, who was away from the office most of the time, never got the picture of the problems that were brewing in the company from her -- nor did he care to hear about them. At first the staff members wanted to discuss their concerns that team issues weren't being addressed, but the president experienced this line of communication as an indication of disloyalty. He saw his employees as being ungrateful for all he was trying to provide for his *troops*. Consequently, without clear communication, the tensions that were building in the group had no where to go.

One staff member, an INTJ, loved to problem solve and build new models for helping the company move forward. These ideas were often rejected by the president. The other staff member was a hard working dedicated INFP who did not feel recognized for his 60 hour work weeks over the course of six years. And the third person was a strong ENFP who couldn't stand to be in an atmosphere of unresolved conflict on a team that she desperately wanted to respect and get back in alignment.

The tension of opposite expectations between hard working staff people and hard working employers could not be resolved because of the context within which conflict was framed. Conflict was held as a destructive source of energy interpreted as disloyalty and a demonstration of disrespect of the president's competencies in running his company. Conflict was also thought of as a destructive tension and was to be avoided at all costs. Problems were expressed from the owners of the business as: "if you're not with me, you're against me."

RESULT

Consequently, the energy and tensions from opposite expectations within the group had no where to go to be expressed and eventually got covertly expressed in the back room by the water cooler. Ultimately, three people left the organization and the residual bad feelings persisted for a long time with each party justifying its position. Sound familiar?

UNDERSTANDING CONFLICT

When a strong Extravert is around a quiet Introvert, the tension of opposite directions for processing information can be experienced quite differently by each: the Extravert often interprets the quietness of the Introvert as stand-offishness. Introverts, on the other hand, often see Extraverts as superficial people who fill the air with a lot of talk.

The Sensing dominant person believes problems are centered around the specifics of what has been said or done. They need to be reminded that there's more to conflict than just the facts. The iNtuitive, however, looks at conflict by focusing on the implications and meaning about what is happening. They need to stick to the issues rather than relate the conflict to the whole picture.

The dominant Thinker may see the dominant Feeler as too touchy-feely. Feelers may see Thinkers as too cold. Thinkers tend to get along better with other Thinkers while Feelers have an easier time getting along with both types because they look for and read others' processes more often. Both Thinkers and Feelers have a difficult time dealing with conflict. Thinking types avoid conflict as an emotional waste of time and Feeling types personalize conflicts.

The strong Judger wants structure and planning when they are involved in activities. The strong Perceiver, however, wants to gather additional information and will want to look at every nook and cranny to be certain they have covered all the possibilities. The inherent tension of these opposites can show up in how jobs and tasks get handled, one person pushing for closure with the other person pulling for possibilities.

If the tension of opposites is the very essence of life itself and without tension there would be no energy and consequently no personality, then the question has to be asked: *"how can we use this pull of opposites to create a win-win model for dealing with conflict as opposed to a win-lose situation that so often exists in organizations?"*

When conflict is viewed as a win-lose situation, the tension between opposite positions can be seen as destructive for team interactions and business results. Conflict as a destructive force creates communication and problem solving strategies that have a "positional" force where decisions are made on a "I win, you lose" basis. This, of course, leads to negative attitudes and disliking of the other person and eventually leads to avoidance of the other person with minimal or primarily formal contact only when required which, of course, leads to more "win-lose" behaviours.

Conflict as a creative force promotes healthy communication and problem solving strategies through constructive "win-win" decision making. This leads to positive feelings, a liking for one another and a seeking out of each other for both informal and formal interactions. This, of course, leads to more "win-win" problem solving decisions.

TWO CRITICAL STEPS FOR MANAGING CONFLICT CONSTRUCTIVELY

The causes of conflict in organizations usually come from one of four sources:

- Differences in how we do things: fast/slow, structured/unstructured, with others/alone.

- Differences in how we view things: important/not important, my values/your values.

- Differences in how we relate to others: interactive/non-interactive, positively/ critically.

- Undefined differences: usually a projection of what Dr. Jung calls our shadow which comes out of our least developed function.

When conflict occurs in the workplace, we are not that tolerant of work styles that are different from our own. The two steps involved in addressing the tensions of opposite functions and the inherent conflict that can exist between people are:

- Understanding the appearances and typical approaches for dealing with conflict.

- Willingness to try new skills for creative conflict management.

APPEARANCES AND APPROACHES FOR DEALING WITH CONFLICT

When problems and conflict exist, the tension that is experienced is focused around two concerns which produce various degrees of positive or negative results in organizations. The two concerns are: a. a concern for one's self and one's position and desires; and   b. the concern for the other party and that person's position and desires. The combinations of these two concerns provides us with four descriptions of conflict and the types of behaviours one might take in attempting to deal with the tension within oneself.

Behaviour #1:   Some people may take an aggressive position due to feeling threatened and therefore reacting to the situation and the people in it. Their behaviours might be loud, argumentative and designed to control the situation around them -- this is a situation where the person's concern is purely for him or herself with little regard for the other person's interest.

This approach would have definite repercussions from people receiving this expression of tension.   The repercussions would be to either take a strong position oneself and fight back, or become quiet and withdraw into oneself leaving the tension unmanaged in either case.

Behavour #2: The approach of reacting by withdrawing from the situation is a demonstration of avoiding the tension and confrontation of the person in front of you. It shows a definite lack of concern both for oneself and for the person who needs to be confronted. Consequently, there is no creative expression of problem solving taking place.

Behavour #3: The third approach is to gloss over the problems and tensions and ignore the tensions by refusing to even consider that there is conflict. This strategy for dealing with conflict is carried out so that people can live in harmony and be "one big happy family". Unfortunately, people power is wasted, people don't grow and develop and the innovative team members often leave the organization to find a more challenging workplace. Pretty much the solution that took place in our case study example.

Behaviour #4: In order to stay in a problem solving mode using the tensions of opposites for creative growth requires that we have the willingness to try new skills by: a. focusing objectively on the problem, b. stating our feelings in a responsible manner by owning our own thoughts and feelings and, c. requesting help from the other person in resolving the tensions that come from the pull of opposite expectations.

These skills ensure that our concerns for our own position and desires are addressed, at the same time recognizing the concerns and desires of the other person involved. An example of this behavour might take the following form:

Step 1. Acknowledge that you have a problem/conflict with the person's behaviour -- not the person. Be specific.

Joe, I feel concerned about the deadline for the program. If the project isn't started soon, I'm concerned we'll be up late again the night before the deadline and I'd rather not do that.

Step 2. Get all the facts.

What are your thoughts on the project deadline? How would you suggest we handle this? What are the consequences from your perspective if we don't get this done on time? What are the benefits to completing it immediately? What is preventing you from working on this project sooner rather than later?

Step 3 Outline your position.

Personally, I feel that I have to take on more of a management role if these patterns for working together on projects aren't addressed and I'd rather not do that.

Step 4. Work out a plan of action each person will take to deal with the problem/conflict and prevent future conflicts. What can I do more of, less of, or differently?

I will take the following steps to help resolve the conflict and prevent future conflicts.

What can the other person do more of, less of, differently?

What steps will the other person take to help resolve the conflict and prevent future conflicts.

Step 5. Set a follow-up meeting.

CONCLUSION

Turn a problem into an advantage by dealing with it in a direct, creative manner. Turn both heads toward problem solving rather than defeating, avoiding, or settling for a less than satisfactory outcome. Like most people, most organizations are less than perfect. Yet, despite personal and organizational flaws, we can improve. If we cannot improve the whole organization, we can improve a division, a department, or perhaps just a few interpersonal relationships.

Somehow, team members' conflict over differences in expectations in the workplace must be combined if an organization is to operate with a positive, creative conflict management approach. When the concern for self and others are combined, the tensions of opposites can be transformed into creating a solid, concrete foundation of understanding.

> *"Many work related problems are nothing more than personality differences out of control. When a person's needs are inappropriate to another person or too strong, they are likely to create significant problems both for that person and for others."* Adapted from Michael E. Cavanagh, University of San Francisco

APPENDIX III

WAYS OF LOOKING AT TEMPERAMENT

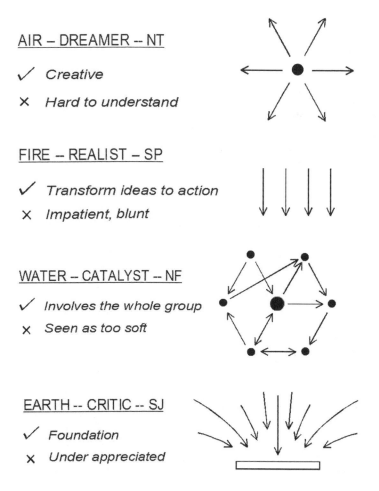

<u>AIR – DREAMER -- NT</u>

✓ *Creative*

✗ *Hard to understand*

<u>FIRE -- REALIST – SP</u>

✓ *Transform ideas to action*

✗ *Impatient, blunt*

<u>WATER – CATALYST -- NF</u>

✓ *Involves the whole group*

✗ *Seen as too soft*

<u>EARTH -- CRITIC -- SJ</u>

✓ *Foundation*

✗ *Under appreciated*

THE WHOLE SYSTEM

NT - Mental Awareness – The Dreamers—IDEAS

Future/Visionary, Optimistic, minded, Unconventional, Creative/Curious, Overflow of Invincible/Strong, Romancing

Inspirational, Open-

Ideas,
Ideas, Alone

SP - Social-Mental Awareness – The Realists—ACTIONS

Bottom-Line Driven, Moving Forward, Don't Like Too Many Details, Crisis/Problem-Solving, Look For Solutions, Appear To Be Leaders, Convincing, Motivating, Appear Insensitive, Looking For What To Do Next, Delegate, Don't Like Conflict, Adaptable, Impatient

NF - Social-Physical Awareness – The Catalyst - REACTIONS

Emotionally Expressive, Connectors, Sensitive, Cautious, Resourceful, Creative Within, Enthusiasm, Intuitive, Caring, Empathetic, Reinventing Themselves, Customer Service, Hosts, Networker, Often Behind the Scenes People

SJ - Physical Awareness – The Critics -- PRODUCT

Problem-Detectors, Analysis, Past Experiences, Perfectionists, Useful, Product-Oriented, Takes Time Before Speaking, Processing Data, Refinement, Practical Quality, Mostly Behind the Scenes People

REFERENCE MATERIALS

Bates, Marilyn & Keirsey, David W. <u>Please Understand Me.</u> Del Mar, CA: Prometheus Nemesis Books, 1978.

Brownsword, Alan. <u>It Takes All Types.</u> San Anselmo, CA: Baytree Publication Company, 1987.

Charlesworth, Edward A. & Nathan, Ronald, PH.D., <u>Stress Management</u>. Ballantine Books, New York

Covey, Stephen R. <u>Principle-Centered Leadership.</u> New York, NY: Fireside, 1990.

Dilts, Robert & Epstein, Todd <u>Tools for Dreamers.</u> Cupertino, CA: Meta Publications, 1991.

Dilts, Robert & G. Bonissone <u>Skills for the Future.</u> Cupertino, CA: Meta Publications, 1993.

Gault, Danielle, <u>Natural To My Soul</u>. Toronto, Ontario, 2000.

Gault, Danielle, <u>The Well-Tempered Life</u>. Toronto, Ontario, D-B Reflections Inc., 2004.

Hunt, Diana & Hait, Pam <u>The Tao of Time.</u> New York, NY: Fireside, 1990.

Kroeger, Otto & Thuesen, Janet M. <u>Type Talk.</u> New York, NY: Delacorte Press, 1988.

ABOUT THE AUTHOR

Danielle Gault, writer, trainer, and natural healer, delivers workshops, coaching and healing services in Ontario, New York, New Zealand and Greece. She has written articles published in the Ontario Association of Psychological Type, local newspapers, Ezine Magazine, Self-Growth website, HR Reporter, and for the Reflexology Association of Canada.

Danielle believes in a holistic approach to living and uses personality theory, natural healing techniques such as Yoga, Reflexology and insightful educational workshops to assist people in addressing their issues in life and striving to live consciously.

Danielle loves sharing her experience with others and is available for corporate training in various topics such as teambuilding, problem solving, assertiveness; she is also available for providing Coaching Certification, Reflexology Certification, or Teachers Training in Reflexology through the Reflexology Association of Canada and through her company, co-founded with her partner Diana O'Reilly.

Have a look at the following websites for more information on courses, products, and services:

www.wellness-training-services.com

www.corporate-training-services.com.

Notes:

_____

_____

_____

_____

_____

_____

_____

_____

_____

_____

_____

_____

_____

_____

_____

_____

_____

_____

_____

Made in the USA
Charleston, SC
03 September 2011